The Year of the Witch

by Shannon Connor Winward

Sycorax Press

Astoria, New York

For my parents, who birthed the witch
for Melinda, who named her thus
and for my children, who show her, mightily,
what magic *is for*...

Text Copyright © 2018 Shannon Connor Winward

Published by Sycorax Press

Astoria, New York

ISBN-13: 978-0-9998839-2-1
ISBN-10:0-9998839-2-5

Covert art by Franetta McMillan

CONTENTS

Introduction   7
How to Read this Book   9

Ostara / Spring   11

Creator   13
Return   15
Chaos Effect   17
Bast   19

Spring Moon Ritual
Prophet   22

Beltane   25

Apotheosis   27
Question   30
Hell's Gardener   31
In Conception   33
Rosemary   35
Prognostication is For the Birds   36

Litha / Summer   37

Midsummer   39
Gardenspew   41
La Petite Mort   42
Breathe   44
My Name is a River   45

Summer Moon Ritual

Gravity   47

Lughnasadh   49

Assembly of One   51
Harvest   53
Getting Wet   54
Atlas, Unhinged   56
The Trout of Senescence   57

Mabon / Autumn   61

Paradox of Return   63
Innocence Elixir   65
Come Kali   67
Arrangement   68

Autumn Moon Ritual

Moon Song   70

Samhain   73

Craving   75
Because I Never Learned to Read the Tarot   76
Thirteen Ways to See a Ghost   77
All Souls' Day   80
Arachne Pending   83
Weaver   85

Yule / Winter   87

Osiris in My Coffee Shop   89
Visitation   90
Paracusia   91
Christmas Eve   94
After the Ice Storm   95

Winter Moon Ritual
Eclipse   97

Imbolc   99

Word-Wright   101
Winter Tanka   102
Cupid's Mark   103
Star-Gazing   104
Undoing Winter   106

Acknowledgments   109
About the Author   113
About the Artist/Scyorax Press   114

Introduction

The Year of the Witch is a circle, not a line.

The Year of the Witch is a map, a record, a story: the Sun's rise and fall; the Moon's wax and wane; the seasons' dance; the parade of stars across our arc of sky.

The Year of the Witch is the echo of what we were told, by fire and lamplight, by cradles, at tables and sickbeds; words made our own now, reborn through our lips as we speak to children. The Year of the Witch is what they will say to their own, in time. It is all they will remember of us.

Time is linear, masculine, a thrusting forward, but the Year of the Witch is feminine; the curve of a belly or breast; the crowning head of a babe; the cup of an outstretched hand. The Year of the Witch is as full or as empty as we find ourselves: a plate; an embrace; an open mouth, womb or grave.

The Year of the Witch is a tool: the round lip of a chalice; the concave mortar; the brimming cauldron; the spinning wheel.

The Year of the Witch is made up of equal parts: some dark, some light, wet or dry, quick or slow, depending on geography in space, on Earth, in mind, and how many times we've taken the ride.

For the purposes of this book, we'll go with four, for seasons, or better yet, eight, to be well-rounded— each divided by an *esbat*, or moon rite, to reflect upon, to remind us of the aforementioned cycles. But know: divisions are always arbitrary. Your measure of the Year is as needful, and needless, as mine.

How to Read this Book

Start where you are. Is it hot outside? Is it raining? Are the first green fingers clawing out of the earth, or are there people in the fields and gardens, sweating, reaping? Are you hungry? Angry? Afraid? Be there.

Or, start where you want to be. Follow your heart. Go backwards. Skip ahead.

Not sure? Unknowing is okay, too. Bibliomancy is as fine an art as any. Pick a page at random: see if there's an answer there, or maybe a question, or even just a needed breath between this moment and another.

Of course, you can to read the book cover to cover, if you choose. There's a story here, though it doesn't matter, really, where it starts and where it ends. It only starts over.

Ostara / Spring

Equinox (from Latin, *aequinoctium*, equality of night and day): an astronomical event (as most beginnings are, to someone, somewhere) in which the Earth divides Herself, twice yearly, in accordance with the Sun's demands (His incessant wandering) and Her own rational alignment.

In the Northern Hemisphere, the March Equinox manifests a Spring, embodied as a Maiden, or a risen ghost, sometimes a hare, or perhaps an egg which, when placed on the sidewalk, will balance on its rounded bottom because of science, faith, magic, or youth's stubborn luck.

To the Witch, Spring is a time of rebirth, growth, and hope: ideal for fertility spells, love charms, or new passion projects.

Correspondences:

Astrological Signs: Aries, Taurus, Gemini

Colors: robin's egg blue, baby cheek pink

dream purple, virgin white, any green

Charms: plastic eggs, birds' nests, bouquets,

paint brushes, galoshes

Scents: rain, soap, fresh-baked bread, newly-turned earth, your mother's perfume

Keyword: Creation

Creator

This was mine.
I said *Begin*
blew a kiss
through my mind
and it was.

I said, *Think*
and it reflected
Me.
I said *Love*
and there was language
talking to itself.

I said *Believe*
and it aligned
Strive
and there was movement
Form
and it began to build
and grow.

There is reason
an axis for chaos
the all-seeing eye
of the storm
a centering ground

an elemental heaven
there is Me

and this
I gave you
this
my surrender
this
was mine, but
what you've done with it—
oh, my darlings
This
was not my doing.

Return

I picked hyacinths with my son
on the way to the car
prizes of pink and purple
in his little fists.
Now I have a bruised bouquet
on my desk at work
in a coffee cup—
their scent heady, cosmetic
making me sneeze

and smile, spreadsheets
forgotten. Hyacinths
are the heralds of rebirth;
after months of cold
and rain and living
boxed up in dry, heated air
a little sprig of color
is serotonin for the soul.

Hyacinths are loyal.
They come back to you
year after year. More generous
than their sister flowers—
forget daffodils, tulips, one-
headed wonders. A hyacinth
has dozens, rows and rows, each
with its mouth open
a Sunday choir

and that thick, syrupy scent
permeates everything so you can't
forget: *Spring! Spring!*
Oh and guess what: Spring.

I did not plant these
hyacinths. My mother did
when the house was hers.
Some from her mother's house
too, return; a reminder that once
she was here.

It is wet outside, and it is hot
in this office, but I am
picking flowers for her. I am
white patent leather shoes
and ribboned hair. I am small
and she is everything. Her skin is cool
powder and perfume, a sweet, cosmetic
scent like hyacinths, and she is *here*
and like earth's promise, will be here
        again.

Chaos Effect

Old lady fiddles with the butterfly pin
come loose from her lapel.

The elevator dings welcome to a level
it's welcomed a million times before.

She steps into the lobby and, distracted, leaves
her coffee on the floor.

But Pele doesn't know this.
She only sees the cup

another piece of litter left to clutter
the vista of her eyes, and

Pele
fumes.

As the elevator rises, Pele conjures
volcanoes in her mind.

What lazy, slovenly infidel
would so dare?

She explodes, later, on her keyboard.
In what universe

is cold, abandoned coffee
reasonable?

It is not really about the coffee
but I don't know this.

I nurse my cup
and soak up her words

my computer screen
begins to simmer

my imagination
rise

my mind opens on a level
it's opened to a million times before, but

in this vista
every time is different.

Maybe this morning
a butterfly fiddles

with the old lady pinned on her lapel
and

before she flies away
she remembers

to pick up her coffee
from the floor.

Bast

She strode through the crosswalk
tucked in smoke-colored fur
snug against the fog
sinking
down
on the pavement.

She made her way through
bodies weaving, almost
careening
into one another, faces
turning to follow.

Caught
at the stop light
I saw my space in traffic
couldn't stop
to confirm
I'd really seen Her.

Caught
in the procession of
cars and people, briefly
out of sync

She moved
with purpose
head high
tail

curled
in a perfect
question:

What if
I thought
eyes darting
from the
rear-view
to the
tail lights—
blink—

rear-view
green arrow
go—
What if
She was more real

than the rest of us
slipping
like runoff through our
engineered channels?

What if
She was
as human, except
in a split-
second glance, revealed

Her true
Goddess
nature?

What if
She'd never
really been there at all
except in the moment
I chose to see

What if
She were
a message
to the Goddess
striding
with purpose
in Me?

Spring Moon Ritual

Prophet

Speak, Sir, and I'll listen—but know, I'll burn
my new moon offerings all the same.
Fool, messiah, lover, brother—you spurn
my new moon offerings all the same.

We talk in code—water of life, oil and grain.
I give, in trade, my secrets.
Careless man, you break them—my heart, my urn,
my new moon offerings all the same.

How you delight in words, denounce idols,
husbands, your clever tongue seeking my
deferential lips and thighs. You yearn
for my new moon offerings all the same.

You take succor at my lap, my well, and tell me
that I thirst. When you leave me for
your spring of truth, I will return
to my new moon offerings all the same.

Heavy is our burden, we who fall for favored sons.
To please Heaven, we draw
the river dry. And yet, in this, we learn
our new moon offerings all the same.

I will not disabuse you, He who, of God's children,
has yet to sacrifice. But know,
on the night you bleed, She'll discern
your new moon offering all the same.

Beltane

One of the four mythic fire festivals of the Celts, Beltane blooms on or about May 1st (halfway between the Vernal Equinox and Summer Solstice).

Known colloquially as May Day, Beltane is a celebration of the fecundity of Nature—Her ever-burning question—as well as its eternal answer in the hearts and loins of (wo)men.

Traditional Beltane rites included the lighting of hearths and bonfires, feasts, festooning doors and wells, sacrifices (symbolic or otherwise), processions, athletic feats of (wo)men and cattle, maypoles, ecstatic dancing, and fornication.

The modern Witch may make use of some or none of these, as befits one's resources and inclination.

Apotheosis

If I take
the moments of my life
tie them to each other
and the axis of experience
perhaps the colors would stream
from heaven, down.

We could each grab a ribbon
and chase our tails
around and
around and

perhaps
in a backwards glance
we might see the Maker there
come to join the procession

to drink the voices
to laugh in the recesses
of our sight
and then
be gone

slipped inside
through the breath
like the presumptuous
spirit He is.

I say, fine.

Let Him in.

I will run faster
on the petals of offerings
I will trail my billows behind me
like a scent.

I will say
catch me if You can

(but don't look back—no
to look in the
face of desire
is to see the spiral).

If You enter me
Sky-Father
You'll find that it gets dark in here.
If You take me, perhaps
I will leave You to stumble
in the caves of the human mind

these tired themes of life
we spin around, and
around.

These memories and colors
will sing You in circles.

Father of Riddles, how You panic

inside what I know.

When You are lost in the pattern, perhaps
I will come inside You
I know well that I can—
You forget, Maker
who made you.

I remember,
having to relearn it every time
a woman bears me. She calls me *daughter*
but You were gone
long before that naming-day.

Perhaps
I will remind You.

Come inside.
When the dawn intrudes
and I rise up from the dirt
my ribbons in shreds under my knees
and You are gone

perhaps, this time
I will have engendered
You.

Question

In the copse of hollow trees
the garrote stole his question, *why*—
Still the maidens smiled, each to each
and explained the hugeness of the sky.

Hell's Gardener
for Julia

There is no sun in Hell
no rain, of course, not even
earth, in the earthly sense, just
a firmament on which to orient
not up from down so much as
then from now
*

and it hurts, of course, it seethes
and burns, breaking the black rock
and digging in, shredding what
once was skin, her damned fingers
worn to nubs, like grinding teeth
*

to gums, like glass
under her spirit nails. Even still,
she's got nothing but time to wrest
surrender, rage open mouths
obsidian cracks, to thumb her fruit
down eternity's throat
*

There are no seeds in Hell
but she came here plump
          as a pomegranate with all the good
she never sowed. She spits her
      stillborn tomorrows, seeps blood pink
                    *

          regret in every hole
and breathes
          intention like prayer, ignites
miasmic air, incites
      hellflowers to bloom
                    *

          There is no life in Hell, of course
but there are gardens
          for her, blossoms of patience
and penitence, pinwheeling rows
      of firedrop petals, blazing yellow hearts,
              and *I'm sorrys* blue as sulfur flames,
      blue as she remembers
                    hope to be
                    *

In Conception

Small things are always dying in my dreams
mice and birds, soft empty skins
a latticework of kittens pulled from baskets
strips of fur and bone

Last night, miniature sea turtles
burrowing in wet cement
octopi clinging to my fingers, living rings
tiny mouths, ten unanswered questions
the same one
       when

The body remembers
the curl of a leg, like a conch shell
tucked to the waist
the tug of a nipple, the weight of it
a being made liquid, love's gravity
       pull, pull

My son grows long, bones stretch
the baby going, gone
a ghost
in the machine. The moon waxes
the body wanes

Your hand on my hip, seeking an opening
the framework pried apart
kisses tidal, ten fingers asking
       when, when

and when I break
I give you everything

The body empty
curls on itself
concave to you, you sleep
I think, *never again*
is enough
but the body remembers, and life proceeds
to dissolve in dreams

Rosemary

When you are gone
I will learn to speak to you
with rosemary.

Every time I kneel before the shrub
your mother gave me
I will think of you.

Every time I worry the soil
I will knead your name
every resentment I will tuck

like a secret
under the roots
where he will never think to look.

With every branch pinched back
crushed and oiled in my palm
this rosemary will be your surrogate.

When you leave, this sacrifice
of friendship for love
will whisper of itself

to the back of my hand:
We used to talk like this...
remember?

Prognostication is For the Birds
For Rebecca

The sparrows on my deck
might be trying to tell me something.
They used to be cool like that, only
the last time, what I thought was an omen
turned out to be just hungry sparrows.
Nothing's changed.

So now I'm like, yeah, whatever sparrows,
eat your birdseed. Except what is or isn't
so important inspired one of them
to dive into the sliding glass door, flailing
like prophecy. Or,
maybe I should put a decal there. I mean,
that's the trouble with augury.
You never can tell.

Litha / Summer

In Latin, *Solstice* tells the story of when the Sun stands still—though of course it does no such thing. To the Witch, the Solstice is a time of paradox and illusion.

In June (on or about the 21st), the Solstice manifests a Summer—and also, elsewhere, Winter. The Sun reaches its zenith, pausing to survey creation while we, Earth's children, collectively, (even ever in motion, and ever alone) stop to hold our breath.

In the north, we call this *Litha,* or *Midsummer,* though also *the Official Start of Summer,* giving ourselves license to wear white sandals, visit swimming pools and festivals, and come fully alive, even as the Sun begins His yearly dying, growing ever less until, in Winter (or Summer), He returns to the dark womb of Heaven to begin again.

Correspondences:

Astrological Signs: Cancer, Leo, Virgo

Colors: ripe-berry red, beach yellow, lust green

Charms: plastic chairs, sea shells, sun discs, nail polish, quill pens, hacky sacks, hemp necklaces

Scents: tomato-on-the-vine, lotion-on-babies, sex

Keyword: Abundance

Midsummer

On August 27, 2003, Earth and Mars converged at a distance of 56 million km— the closest perihelic opposition since Earth's prehistory.

June is living on without you,
wet with mist and wanting open
the fruit of too-long winter still small
and tight against the vine.

The plans I made in tatters, our tomorrows
woven in my lap
to swaddle daughters;
it doesn't take a husband to make life.

Hope is kicking in my belly, blood singing
in my womb. I can give myself to long, warm
nights.

July has been weeping for us
stars drawn up behind pinked clouds
but Mars is brushing against the Earth
nearer than fifty-thousand years.

This pain of children breaks your composure
my heart aches like an old battle wound.

Magic is going to happen
the planets know it, and so do I.
August is moving on without you, and I think
my darling, I am going too.

Gardenspew

the garden was afoot
how many volcanoes
when it bloomed
seeding like wasps at war
the pomp and circumstance
of fruit flies
aggrandizing
always, always
their insistent nothings
their dappled dreams

La Petite Mort

I am not asleep
         on a plastic-wrapped mattress
                  in my living room

                  pale sun leering
         through venetian
blinds

         lack of air-
                  conditioning sticking to a
         familiar suicide

as the
         summer
                  slips
                           by

                           muttering
                  in the wake
         of a fan
for days

         living
                  like always
                           by the whim of the
                  weather

(If he really loved me
         he wouldn't cry)

The sheets give up

        their weak little grip
flushed naked skin
        saran-wrapped insides

                                sick

        with the *crinkle*
of plastic
        beneath my thighs
                convulsing
                        unremarkably

        these little deaths
        in tissues
tumbled
on the
        floor.

Breathe

I am charcoal lozenges
the clearing of the throat
a wiggling haunch of cat, never yet pouncing
the coffee cool before I can swallow
mercury
thirteen reasons why
a crackedback chair, but beloved
earth blue cushion, worn thin
a mouthful of juice marrow, blood, orange and
stars
my belly overturned, a bucket, beating sticks
yesterday, today echoes, today, today, tomorrow
I am wave after wave
calling the ocean from here but wait, only
wet with rain, the concrete womb-warm
and grit under my toes
yew berries, pluck and slip
the mist, the point, the scythe
the menses of summer
tomorrow
July sighs in, out. in. It is all right
if it never comes
again

My Name is a River*

Today it is Pain
same as yesterday
same as tomorrow.

Once it was Storm
blue stubborn of sorrow
before that maybe sunbird Yellow

but always also
Shade, under, always
where light and dark things meet,

become. Once I was One
now I am Several, him and me
but Them, mostly.

My name, I Forget.
My name means littlewise—
there's a story to it, but I don't have

Time to tell you. Time
is a river; look—
I keep going

without ever leaving
or else always coming back.
But I was here

before You
and I'll be here after you're gone.
I am The Place where all pain goes

this is what I was named to do:
I move the tears of Heaven
to the waiting hands of The Sea.

*The name Shannon derives from Sionainn, an Irish
goddess who drowned in the waters of divine wisdom;
She is the namesake and patron of the longest river in
Ireland and all of the most westerly islands of Europe.

Summer Moon Ritual

Gravity

What I do not tell you
could draw down moons.
Sometimes I think it transcends words, anyway.
Words are only a means of explaining things, like
gravity
Yes, of course, gravity is why the
water always comes back
to the shore.
It's all perfectly
scientific.

Perfectly.

I wonder if the ocean beats herself up
for feeling this way.

Lughnasadh

The second of the Celtic fire festivals, Lughnasadh (*LOO-na-sa*) falls roughly upon August 1st—midway between the Summer Solstice and the Autumnal Equinox. Patterns and balance allow us to feel less like vulnerable accidents, more like gods.

Lughnasadh is named in honor of the Irish god Lugh, who embodies the most superlative of (wo)men's aspirations: virility, prowess, cleverness, artistry, and mastery of useful trades.

A celebration of the first harvest, Lughnasadh is traditionally celebrated with more of what party people do best: gatherings, competitions, theatrics, roasting of sacrificial delectable beasts, inebriation and feasts, matchmaking, lovemaking, and merrymaking of all sorts.

Lughnasadh rites often feature sympathetic magic with first agricultural products: altars heaped with vegetables, fruit, and bread, gifts of goodies to the fickle fae folk, and crafts of braided straw. Corn dollies fastened in the likeness of goddess mothers symbolize gratitude for Earth's bounties and ward against starvation, sickness, and other misfortunes that lurk in the shadows of an inevitable Winter.

Assembly of One

I pull the stalks up with my hands
venturing shoeless from the strip
of weekly-mown grass
into the wilderness of nettle
thorns and glass.

I break the stems with my bare hands
nails torn ragged
to sever summer's growth.
The skin is worn away as I reap
a bundle of reeds and wildflowers.

I wave away seeds and insects
knock loose their grip—
tiny bodies scatter on my skirt.
The sun burns my back
from a suburban sky
neatly painted within the lines of houses.

White aluminum siding ripples and falls back.
Housewives watch from window steam.
My harvest, weeds clutched in bleeding palms
like quills with peasant's ink.
My bundle, grain from another life—
I recreate the Cradle.

Another feast day passing quietly
I leave the assembly of one

and pick my way back to my concrete porch
with the gifts of earth and sun; an offering
from the bounty of the year
to be molded in the likeness of the Mother—

A twist of braids, limbs and leaves
crowned and ribboned and hung from my door
'til the fields lie folded under frost and wind
and the Lady of winter comes knocking
leaving in her passing seeds for new life
to be reaped in their own time
with my love-worn hands.

Harvest

a mother opens
an ear of corn, unravels
in sticky little hands

Getting Wet

The first time I tasted
sweet plum wine
was like kissing a girl
with a candy tongue
deep between her satin sheets

The first time I kissed a girl
was like sliding into
a black velvet dress
that perfectly mirrored
my curves and lengths

The first time I wore
a black velvet dress
was like hearing my mother
invoke me (shiver-clear
as seven-up and gin
in a glass in a smoky room) but not
by the name I was given

The first time I took a name
of my own choosing
I thought I was deep
like the baby sprinkled at the
baptismal font thinks it's drowning
having no frame of reference

The first time I drowned
my mouth filled with brine, rank

and sour as my grandfather's spit
tobacco, it was the first
of many betrayals

up and down switching places
without warning, the boardwalk Gravitron ride
spinning suddenly not fun but sick with motion
and weight and headache-inducing depth
like the third glass
of sweet plum wine

like the girl, the dress, the name
the ocean, more satisfying this side of wisdom
when you know what you're getting
yourself into
and you get in *anyway*

Atlas, Unhinged

Radical insolence
the stars flaunt their light
though I have called for all the world
to close its eye.
I am in pain. You all
need to stop
what you are doing
I cannot bear it, the earth
spinning on
my shoulders host to an orgy of
candor, life
proceeding
the universe dazzling and
applauding
as if the way I feel means,
in the scheme of things,
little. *Stop.*
I could let go. I mean it,
if I were crushed
between heaven and
this
could it hurt
any less? At least then I could
for a moment
hold my own heart
while it breaks.
Don't push me, damn it, I said

be still
leave me my grief
and look away.

The Trout of Senescence

is a slippery bitch
thoughts cast and snagged
a flop of the tongue
the meaning of things, gone
in a shiver, a crick
in the neck

a flash of silver
at the brow, the crotch
of dark waters
creeping up
while we wait on lines

the nagging twitch
the too-stiff grip, fingers fret-
ful as knots
in a net

things fall apart
things sag, empty
tear and gap
things drip

and disappear
like daybreak, the bloodgold
dulled gray as cancer
yet another morning
the quickening pulse

slowed, the flaccid
thump of life

drowning on the dock
bare feet on the floorboards
from here, boy
everything goes downstream

Mabon / Autumn

Equinox (from Latin, *aequinoctium*, equality of night and day): an astronomical event, as are most realizations of *yes:* haven't we been here before?

In the Northern Hemisphere, the September Equinox manifests an Autumn, embodied as an apple, a scythe, a Forest God in his pied plumage, or the approaching specter of Death, undoing.

The second Celtic harvest festival, Mabon heralds a return to classrooms and other fields, inventories of jars and cans, consequences; a sober moment, perhaps, between the largess of Summer and the quick descent to Winter's want.

To the Witch, Autumn is a time of reflection, plans, and winnowing: ideal for binding spells, health charms, or making lists.

Correspondences:

Astrological Signs: Libra, Scorpio, Sagittarius

Colors: school supply red, trump orange, moon yellow, compost brown, dying green

Charms: plastic pumpkins, scissors, acorns, apple seeds, rakes, brooms, jars

Scents: bonfire smoke, spice, rotting leaves, basements, fresh-baked pie, your father's cologne

Keyword: Collection

Paradox of Return

The tilt of the earth
is 23 ½ degrees
It is fixed in space
but it whirls.

                    We don't change
                    but we will.

The axis is always
parallel to itself
as it leans to
and turns from the sun.

                    I push and you pull
                    but no one has won.

Summer dawns
simultaneous to winter
Night never rises
as day never sets.

                    When you wake
                    I am sleeping.

The fate of the globe
is an ellipsis
one solstice never more than
5 million kilometers from another.

Opposites cannot exist
without each other.

The procession of time
is an imperfect circle
What falls back springs forward
and ends where it started.

If you wait for it to right
itself you'll wait forever.

Twice a revolution
the gift of light is everywhere equal
Exactly twice there is balance
in the tides of the year.

What we push away
we can draw near.

As the world turns, once daily
by right of paradox
tomorrow and yesterday
are everywhere the same.

What we have ended
we can begin again.

Innocence Elixir

Begin with:
> The cauldron of a woman's body, ~~much~~
> ~~used~~   seasoned

Brace with:
> Scrap wood
> Yard waste
> A day's work

Invite the neighbors:
> to witness the kindling
> Strike, light, be awed
> Relax

Infuse with:
> 1 can Budweiser, then another (Repeat)
> 2 hands English Leather (or Chaps,
>> or old-fashioned sweat, but never
>> *Drakkar Noir.* This will ignite her,
>> and sour the concoction.)
>
> Half a pack of cigarette ash (brand
>> irrelevant, she doesn't remember)

Incant, for hours:
> Politics
> Polack jokes
> *Danny Boy* (or Jim Croce)

Insert ~~sticks~~ wands until hot, glowing. Swirl
vigorously. Spell her name in sparks.

Once reduced to her purest essence:
        lift her high.
        Brush with 1 man
                unshaven
                cheek-to-cheek

Convince her:
        A star in heaven burns cherry red
                just for her, and
        the future is everything Daddy promised
                it could be

Come Kali

Her dark
lips
grasping
blood
tongue
lapping
swallowing
    one tower
whole
then
the other
comes Kali.
Fire licks
the steel
sticks
free of ants
free of souls

O Comes
Kali.
Her
black arms
sweep
Babel's
streets
plucking
children
screaming
    to Her
breast—
the Great
Mother
suckles
us
breathless.

Arrangement

Across the table
she's plucking petals from the nasturtiums.
They taste like cinnamon
and stick to her tongue.
They burn like kisses
she'll never tell you of.

Outside it's raining.
October comes in that way—
cold and gray
but across the table she's swallowing fire
dripping wax through her teeth
a jack-o-lantern smile
yes, and yes, and oh, the weather.

She covers her wrists
with the heels of her sweater. Pulled tighter
you can't see the scars
or the supernovas
whorls of Van Gogh suns spiraling
kamikaze under her breast
as she watches her decaf
coffee steam.

She concurs,
head and shoulders and backbone bent
pleasantries leaning inward
sunflowers left too-long untended

top-heavy and old.

Her spirit smolders
but your kitchen is cool
and quiet
and she sighs, perched like still life
across the table.

Moon Song

Sometimes, when I am driving
and the moon hangs fat in the sky
like it did last night
I can sing a song to wake the dead.

I don't know if it's me casting the spell
or the spell casting me
I just know that the song rises
like the ocean reaching for the sky

and I sing until my voice cracks
as I pull into the driveway
and when my voice fades
there is an echo.

I don't know if it's something that I did
or something that happens to me
but I sang the dead awake last night, and I think
they followed me home

because now I have ghosts dancing inside me.
Their steps are loud enough
to wake the living
and I am shaken

but I don't know what song to sing
to send them back to sleep again.

Samhain

The third Celtic fire festival and final harvest celebration coincide in Samhain (*SOW-in*), known alternately as All Saint's Eve or Hallowe'en (October 31st). Samhain is also recognized by some as the Witches' New Year, due to its liminal position between the Autumnal Equinox and the Winter Solstice—a transitional period when the business of living is all but put aside (cattle and children brought in from pasture, larders and garages as full as they will get) and the long wait of Winter looms upon the doorstep.

As at Beltane and Lughnasadh, Samhain is met with blazes—this time to bless and protect the homestead with the light of faith to last the darkest months of the Year. The ancients offered goods to placate gods, fae, and wandering spirits, just as we do today. The rite of costumed mummery is said to confuse ill-intentioned and chaotic forces by helping us blend in. Safely masked against our true nature, we might frolic and make merry, even in the shadow of the scythe.

To the Witch, Samhain is a time of high magic and possibility; with the veil between the worlds worn thin, one might invite passed-over loved ones for a meal, lay a tarot spread or scry—through smoke and candlelight, mirrored reflections, or coffee steam—to days and passages yet to come.

Craving

ghosts

try not to scream

(a cup of tea
or steam)

the peculiar have
their reasons

even now
the weight of loss

erasure poem from Graveminder, *Melissa Marr*

Because I Never Learned to Read the Tarot

*(after Rod Jellema's "Because I Never
Learned the Names of Flowers")*

It is candlelight and velvet where
I smudge away the bitter-mocha mad mojo funk
and motion for you to belly-up to my tableau.
I flex the deck into an artful bridge and begin
to delvesee into your destiny
the whole esoteric assemblage of Truth.

Seeker, I scry for you
Cacophony and The Sycophant, crisscross the King
of Irony. The Waiting Uber

Below, Astonishment above; the Queen
of Tablecloths covers you. As others see you,
Ambivalence. Happenstance, your hopes and fears.
The Apogee. The Trump.

I prophecy Five Fisticuffs, I divine Nine disastrous
Tweets; the Bearer of Mufflers, Bravado, The Coffee
Shop, and the Ace of Bases,

oracling: the Scissors, the Knight of Whenevers,
your best course of action. Sustenance, the
Dilettante. The Wheel of Dissonance.

Thirteen Ways to See a Ghost

1.

As a young woman, your mother finds a dead
uncle watching her sleep. The chair is no longer
wedged against the door.

2.

Neighbors tell her the couple who owned this
house first lost a child. Your mother found him.
The crayon marks in her closet could have come
from her own, but she sees him, not much taller
than the mattress, circumnavigating the bed, as
children do, while your father and the boys are
sleeping.

3.

You make a joke of it, but he bit her once, left
marks, and how would you explain that?

4.

There's a closet under the basement stairs, a perfect
Bat Cave and hiding place. *Not-it* once, your
brother hears, distinctly, *Hi*. He forfeits the game.

5.

You never found him, but you've lost enough in
that closet.

6.

Your mother cleans the Hazard house, a squat
yellow colonial leftover spitting distance from the
old capitol with roots under the New Castle
cobblestone. It reeks of piss and centuries. The
basement stairs are narrow, dank. She prefers to
leave it to the cats until one she's never seen before
climbs out and growls, *Get out.* After that, she
makes the owner leave the *Mop-n-Glo* upstairs.

7.

"I'm supposed to be here," she spits back. "*You* get
out."

8.

You do the Garrett mansion by the Pennsylvania
border, too, when it's still a school. Your job
is to flip chairs for the boys, collect bits too big for
the vacuum mouth. You visit the animals, nose to
their cedar-lined cages, and the human skull, and
play outside on the hill alone. You don't remember
the house, just the trees and open sky, the town of
Yorklyn sleepy and rustling below, but Mom says
those basements go deeper than any should. There
are three, one under the next, and no one is allowed
to go past the first. Slaves slept down there. It's
darker than dark, and what breathes out at you is
not about freedom.

9.

Your grandfather slept in the basement until your

mother kicked him out for whoring, and then he died. You don't remember him, either.

10.

In second grade you start a ghost club. You hold hands over the drainage grates at recess (because the dead prefer damp, dark places) and tell lost souls to move on. The other girls swear they can see them too.

11.

In the basement of your parents' house, your bags are packed. You are used to things sitting on the mattress, tugging the sheets, but that is no Casper-friendly child. That is man-sized. It is an absence of light, still there when you click on the lamp, but not after you scream. It doesn't want you to go.

12.

You worked nights at the old school below where the Garrett house burned down. A caretaker haunts it, walking the halls, rustling papers, shutting doors—but this story is not about you.

13.

When they escort your parents to the room where your brother's body lies waiting, your mother stammers, "I've never met anyone who died," which, by any definition, just isn't true.

All Souls' Day

The tree has lost her colors early
but she remembers me
she murmurs under my hands
and opens her arms wide

I crawl into her lap
I whisper my name
I pull my sweater tighter
against November's sky

Her bony branches snare
a canopy of mists
if the veils can ever part
it would be now

and here, where the ground
holds my stones,
my stories
like little unmarked graves

It takes a certain alchemy
an arrangement of bones
crisscross, in a cradle of wood
bark, soil, flesh, and stone

If I close my eyes, I can feel them
drawn like spirits to light
a fairy-ring of once-was girls
a circle of the ghosts of me

One in pigtails
one with scars
one who bangs her fists
upon the bark

She gathers blossoms
she gathers wishes
she weaves resentments
like a crown

She wields twigs like swords
she reads sheltered from the sun
she wraps her pain in snakeskin
and buries it among the roots

I hear her singing, praying
I know her thoughts
I live again her promise
to leave the past behind

but I know what she is
too young to understand
all selves are fleeting
and tomorrow never comes

Each day I have to bury
the one who came before
each night I make way for
another me yet to be born

She won't be the one to
overcome it. She is long gone
but if ever the way to her is
open, it would be *this*.

It takes a certain frame of mind
memories gathered, a joining of hands

on the day of all souls, briefly
we are whole again.

Arachne Pending

Sticky cords spun around my wrists
and throat   wrapped

stuck
in the threads of the Weaver.

Her web a warm, snug prison
every time the wind blows, I sway

It will all be
okay.

I am dancing
above the ground

my body pulses,   silk
gestating in my belly

pain is invisible   perfect
seeping from my

chastened fingers, humbled joints
blessed even to tie a knot

let alone a symphony, touch
a blade of grass

a telephone pole
waiting
to tell you I understand now
Lady   what beauty is.

Weaver

Do you think that the spider
thinks of her thread-making
any more than the woman
thinks of her tears?

It is a part of her body.
It just comes.

When she has to search for
the right kind of fiber,
she should know
it is not the time to sew.

Her art is not about the substance—
it is all in the picking
and in the tying to her landscape
she does
in accordance with the reason
of her nature.

When the spider thinks,
she thinks of weaving. Her knowledge
is wrapped up in filaments
she is compelled to bind together.

Her creation is more than merely an act of love.
It is an act of survival.

But when she has to question why
she should spell her life in patterns
she should know
it is not the time for telling.

Her task is not about the context—
it is all in the webbing
and the teasing out
of tangles
she is constantly gestating
in the belly of her mind.

Do you think that the words
dream of their ensnaring
any more than the web
dreams itself undone?

It is a part of the cycle.
It just comes.

When the winds pull at her bindings
and the strands take flight
she should know
it is time to spin again.

Her work is not about completing—
it is all in the unfolding
and the urgency of beauty
she is always heeding
in accordance with the structure
of her soul.

Yule / Winter

Once more, the drama paradox of Heaven climaxes in December (on or about the 21st); the Solstice manifests a Winter—and also, somewhere, Summer.

In the north, the dying god has met His end—and also His beginning. From the depth of darkness He is reborn—emerging, growing, surging towards the vigor of a promised Spring. We call this *Yule*, or *Christmas*, or *Midwinter*, though also *the Official Start of Winter*, giving ourselves license to hold on just a little longer, for even in our darkest moment we know *this too shall pass*.

Correspondences:

Astrological Signs: Capricorn, Aquarius, Pisces

Colors: menses red, frost white, promise green

Charms: plastic wreaths, boughs, icicles, glitter, candles, stockings, shovels

Scents: pine resin, chimney smoke, fresh-baked cookies, coming snow

Keyword: Perseverance

Osiris in My Coffee Shop

I look up from my papers
As always, I am unprepared for you

the way I tend to grow towards you
my worth sinking and rising on your entrance

and it is only in this instant
the word *sustainable* on the page in flames

that I remember this dream
and find it curious

I dressed you in an overcoat
You are ever out of place

my sister-brother, where I am
your brown arms naked heart embracing full

me scrambling to pick up pieces—
silly. Could you just imagine? You

come to sow anything
in my Mid-Atlantic winter.

Visitation

A flickering woke me from half-trance
a Solstice candle left burning
now a coil of flames
snakelike, silver paint peeling, reeking
smoke, crone fingers
reaching. I had to snuff her out
rapture giving way to
fear like autumn
to winter, light
to dark. I turned on the lamp
the room full of clouds.
Now the windows are gaping
the summer fan spinning
the night after Yule
sending silver smoke sliding
out across the snow.

Paracusia

1.

Sometimes voices wake me from my dreams
and follow me throughout the day

> déjà vu
> a record, skipping.

Considered alone
their conversation is innocuous

> *Libraries are westerly.*
> *Throw out the chicken.*

but as a lingual bridge
from dream to reality

> *iloveyouiloveyou*
> *wait!*

I can't shake the notion
that I should wake up

> and pay attention.

2.

I drew my bedspread
across a burning candle

and caught the edge on fire.

As I tried to put it out
an old woman stood over my shoulder
insisting I was doing it wrong

so I began to blow
great, desperate puffs of air
but the flames engulfed the bed.

> *For Godssake,*
she shouted.
> *Stop breathing.*

> 3.

Sometimes I wake up gasping.

> 4.

Our bedroom was brighter when I woke
than it was when I fell asleep.

I searched every room.
I checked the ashtray.

I collapsed beside my husband
but struggled against sleep

convinced that if I drifted off
the fire would become real

the house would fill with smoke
and I would die

curled around his body in a rigid *s*
as he snored and dreamed of things

that stay where they belong.

Christmas Eve

they dressed you with needles
threaded tubing through you
bound your hands and feet
and left the curtains wide

for all to see
your gown up to your belly
mound, vulva, knees
askew, your soiled sheets

as you twisted and thrashed
fighting ammonia dreams
your organs shutting down
like your firstborn, slumped

at the kitchen table
sleeping off his heroin
while the rest of us struggled
with what they'd given you,

the most generous
odds of life.

After the Ice Storm

she sees the driveway as a bleached harbor

her husband gloved and muffled
chipping the truck carcass

his breath like chimes
dripping from woolen scarf and beard

reminds her of her father

an old man
in another house
enduring as if he were alive,
dreaming of her brothers, addicted boys
never to dig out
or walk out again

she is forgiving her tongue
having slept splintered
pretending at epiphany

> suffering
> does not undo suffering
> hospice is the prerogative of the young

she sees this
arrangement more tidal
and frosty than death

that last finality

brazen-drunk

as a sibling
eternally forging Grief
in the family

she sings, while she nurses the children
tomorrow's custodian of graves
sees herself
ignoring
all arcs to him—

but a brief trip
blackened field husks
beside the highway
all that unswept ice
at his door

Winter Moon Ritual

Eclipse

Your Hecate disc
dark pendant goddess swings
between the mass of you

and the tract of me.
Make it hard I say
(so I can feel).

You shake your head
fearful of what monsters
might come

as (Hecate falls in my mouth)
you thrust
(where I am weak).

So why is it when I tell you
I am (scared) done and push
away

you think
to bare your teeth
and bite my breast

(and this
you do not mention)
is okay?

After, you sleep as (he slept) men do,
snoring, unbroken
moon dreams

while I cover (give birth to)
things swollen, things
women know

curled up
in the corner
on the floor.

Imbolc

The last of the Celtic fire festivals (or perhaps the first, depending where you are in the turn of this Year) lights the midway point between the Winter Solstice and the Spring Equinox. Imbolc (*im-Bolg, "in milk"*) heralds the birth and lactation of livestock as well as the quickening in the hearts and hands of (wo)men—a time of renewed activity and purpose.

Imbolc fires are productive fires: clearing out dark, cobwebbed corners, illuminating the path from stable to door, or porch light to headlights, prayers and thanksgiving for a dawn that comes ever sooner—and with it, Spring.

As the name suggests, traditional Imbolc rituals featured dairy products as sympathetic magic: a splash of milk on the ground, or perhaps an extra dab of butter on toast to encourage the fattening of the land. Yet even the lactose-intolerant Witch has no shortage of rites to choose from: the Celtic goddess Brigid, patron of farmers and husbandry, mothers and midwifery, poets, artists, smiths, Irish Catholics, wells, rolling green places, forges, hearths, and all things fiery is also honored on this day. Ribbons and straw crafts made in Her likeness during harvest might be dusted off and placed in sacred places such as altars, workstations, doors, kitchen arches, bed sheets and cradles.

Word-Wright

Like any good Brigid's daughter
I am trying to tend the flame
in these drafty hallways—
a tiny little thing.

I am cupping my fingers around an ember
but the wind keeps trying to take it
and the dead leaves of autumn
come scampering across my floor.

Like any good Bride's daughter
I am trying to forge new words
my fingers are liquid heat
in memory of touching you

but life unborn is still, yet, sleeping
in the ground
and the chill of winter
is knocking at my door.

Winter Tanka

First snow of the year
melts from pink boots alongside
the heating vent as
my daughter smiles, sporting
a cocoa goatee

Cupid's Mark

Monday, I told Mother about the strange pain
between my shoulders.

She said, "Maybe you're growing wings."

But by Thursday, the pain had travelled
to just under the scapula.

Sometime last night, it penetrated my heart.

Now it sticks like an arrow through my left breast.
I keep touching it

surprised when my fingers come back clean.
I think maybe she was onto something

if love is like a phantom limb
that aches after it's gone.

Star-Gazing

Talk to me again.
Speak slowly
and use

very

big

words.

I want to coax
your voice
from your tongue.

I want to rasp together
taste buds
and make a song

seductive and unexpected
as crickets
under the winter sky.

I want to shout
and startle the stars
make them fall like snowflakes.

I want to know the taste
of crystal constellations
clear as our infatuation

but I bite my lip
and turn to remark
on the absence

of Gemini.

Undoing Winter

I went into ground for you. I faced the guardians
of the gates of hell.
I gave away my jeweled bracelets
and marched naked to the catcalls of the dead
all to rescue your sorry ass
and here you are,
huddled on your mildewed throne
speechless as a shrug.

I faced the shining wrath of the sun
on your behalf
while you cried your soul away.
I made excuses to the earth and sky
and fed the peasants gravel.
Give it time, I said. She is composting.
Come again tomorrow.

But there's been seven years of darkness, darling.
Time enough to conquer demons
with your gentle heart.
We all know how lovely
your sorrow can be, we know how well this dim
underlight becomes you.
But open your eyes, love. Behold your kingdom.
You are just an idol of fungus here,
Sovereign queen of basements.

I wrote this song for you, dearheart.
I went to all this trouble.

Now I'm standing before you and my feet are cold
in fact I'm fucking freezing.
So get your coat.
It's a long way to the light and I am leaving
and you are coming with me.
There will be no more discussion
because I will not waste my breath.
I need it to sing you home.

When we get there, I'm going to take
a long, hot bath
to wash away this grime.
Then we'll have tea and cake
on the veranda
and we will speak of spring.
Until then, I don't want to see your face.

You can write sonnets, if you like,
in praise of the Lord of Shadows.
Paint some stormy watercolors.
Invent a flower.
I don't really care
so long as you get started
undoing this winter that you created.

ACKNOWLEDGMENTS

Many thanks to the editors of the publications in which the following poems appeared, sometimes in slightly different forms:

EMG-Zine, "Creator" (January 2011)
Hip Mama Zine, "Return" (Published as "Hyacinths") (December 2011)
Eye to the Telescope, "Chaos Effect" (January 2016)
Eternal Haunted Summer, "Bast" (December 2012)
The Queen of the Sky Who Rules Over All the Gods (Bibliotheca Alexandrina), "Bast" (reprint, May 2015)
The Ghazal Page, "Prophet"(December 2013)
NewMyths.com, "Apotheosis" (December 2011)
Songs of Eretz Poetry Review, "Apotheosis" (reprint, June 2015)
NewMyths.com, "Hell's Gardener" (June 2017)
Star*Line, "Question" (April 2017)
Gargoyle, "In Conception" (March 2017)
Elementary... My Dear (Kind of a Hurricane Press), "Rosemary" (published as "Remembrance") (December 2015)
Mirror Dance, "Midsummer" (June 2014)
Quail Bell Magazine, "Breathe" (May 2017)
Undoing Winter (Finishing Line Press), "Gravity" (2014)
Dreamstreets, "Assembly of One" (published as "Lughnasadh") (Fall 2015)
The Cicada's Cry, "Harvest" (June 2015)
The Monarch Review, "Getting Wet" (January 2017)
Eternal *Haunted Summer*, "Atlas, Unhinged" (March 2015)
Astropoetica, "Paradox of Return" (July 2012)

Eternal Haunted Summer, "Come Kali" (December 2012)

The Dark Ones: Shadow Gods Anthology (Bibliotheca Alexandrina), "Come Kali" (November 2016)

Apiary, "Arrangement" (December 2011)

Bette Noire, "Moon Song" (October 2012)

Undoing Winter (Finishing Line Press), "Moon Song" (2014)

The Science Fiction Poetry Association Poetry Contest, "Craving" (First place winner, short poem category, 2016)

Silver Blade, "Because I Never Learned to Read the Tarot" (May 2017)

The Science Fiction Poetry Association Poetry Contest, "Thirteen Ways to See a Ghost" (Second place winner, long poem category, 2016)

Jack-O'-Spec: Tales of Halloween and Fantasy (Raven Electrick Ink) "All Souls' Day" (2011)

Spec-tacular: Fantasy Favorites from Raven Electrick Ink, "All Souls' Day" (2012)

The 2012 Rhysling Anthology, "All Souls' Day"

Eternal Haunted Summer, "Arachne, Pending" (March 2015)

Undoing Winter (Finishing Line Press), "Weaver" (2014)

Three Drops From a Cauldron, "Visitation" (December 2015)

Eclectica Magazine, "Paracusia" (January 2013)

Eclectica Magazine Best Poetry Volume One, "Paracusia" (December, 2016)

Thirteen Myna Birds, "Eclipse" (August 2016) *Sagewoman*, "Word-Wright" (November 2012)

Eternal Haunted Summer, "Cupid's Mark" (March 2016)

Blood and Roses: A Devotional Anthology in Honor of Aphrodite (Bibliotheca Alexandrina), "Cupid's Mark" (July 2017)

Apiary, "Star-Gazing" (September 2011)
Undoing Winter (Finishing Line Press), "Undoing
   Winter" (2014)

About the Author

Shannon Connor Winward is a Delaware writer of speculative fiction and poetry. She is the author of the Elgin-award winning chapbook, *Undoing Winter* (Finishing Line Press, 2014) and winner of the 2018 Delaware Division of the Arts Emerging Artist Fellowship in Fiction. Her work has appeared in *Fantasy & Science Fiction, Analog, Gargoyle, Qu, Psuedopod's* Artemis Rising Series, *The Pedestal Magazine, Lunch Ticket, Minola Review, Eternal Haunted Summer, The Monarch Review, Literary Mama, Eternal Conversation, PANK, Flash Fiction On-line, Strange Horizons,* and *Heiresses of Russ: The Year's Best Lesbian Speculative Fiction,* among others. In between writing, parenting, and other madness, Shannon is also a poetry editor for *Devilfish Review* and founding editor of *Riddled with Arrows Literary Journal.* Visit Shannon on the web at www.ShannonConnorWinward.com.

About the Artist

Franetta McMillan is a writer and digital artist who divides her time between Newark, Delaware and Avondale, Pennsylvania. Her poetry, short stories, essays, and illustrations have appeared in *Dreamstreets*, *The Broadkill Review*, and other print and online publications. She is the author of *Love, War and Music*, a poetry chapbook; *What We Saw in the Fire*, a collection of short stories; *Under an Alien Moon*, a book of digital photography; and *Love in the Time of Unraveling*, a novel.

About Sycorax Press

Sycorax Press is a small press devoted to speculative poetry, focusing on fantasy. To learn more, please visit us at www.sycoraxpress.com.

www.ingramcontent.com/pod-product-compliance
Lightning Source LLC
Chambersburg PA
CBHW051814040426
42446CB00007B/672